Improving Dispute Resolution for California's Injured Workers

EXECUTIVE SUMMARY

Nicholas M. Pace • Robert T. Reville • Lionel Galway • Amanda B. Geller
Orla Hayden • Laural A. Hill • Christopher Mardesich • Frank W. Neuhauser
Suzanne Polich • Jane Yeom • Laura Zakaras

Prepared for the
California Commission on Health and Safety
and Workers' Compensation

RAND
INSTITUTE FOR CIVIL JUSTICE

The research described in this report was prepared for the California Commission on Health and Safety and Workers' Compensation. This research was conducted by the RAND Institute for Civil Justice.

Library of Congress Cataloging-in-Publication Data

Improving dispute resolution for California's injured workers /
Nicholas M. Pace ... [et al.]
    p. cm.
    "MR-1425."
    Includes bibliographical references.
    ISBN 0-8330-3276-3 (pbk.)
    1. California. Workers' Compensation Appeals Board—Rules and practice. 2. Workers' compensation claims—California. 3. Workers' compensation—Law and legislation—California. I. Pace, Nicholas M. (Nicholas Michael), 1955–

    KFC592.2 .I47 2003
    344.794'021—dc21

                                                                    2002156096

    "MR-1425/1."
    ISBN 0-8330-3348-4

RAND is a nonprofit institution that helps improve policy and decisionmaking through research and analysis. RAND® is a registered trademark. RAND's publications do not necessarily reflect the opinions or policies of its research sponsors.

Cover design by Stephen Bloodsworth

Published 2003 by RAND
1700 Main Street, P.O. Box 2138, Santa Monica, CA 90407-2138
1200 South Hayes Street, Arlington, VA 22202-5050
201 North Craig Street, Suite 202, Pittsburgh, PA 15213
RAND URL: http://www.rand.org/
To order RAND documents or to obtain additional information,
contact Distribution Services: Telephone: (310) 451-7002;
Fax: (310) 451-6915; Email: order@rand.org

THE INSTITUTE FOR CIVIL JUSTICE

The mission of the RAND Institute for Civil Justice (ICJ) is to improve private and public decisionmaking on civil legal issues by supplying policymakers and the public with the results of objective, empirically based, analytic research. The ICJ facilitates change in the civil justice system by analyzing trends and outcomes, identifying and evaluating policy options, and bringing together representatives of different interests to debate alternative solutions to policy problems. The Institute builds on a long tradition of RAND research characterized by an interdisciplinary, empirical approach to public policy issues and rigorous standards of quality, objectivity, and independence.

ICJ research is supported by pooled grants from corporations, trade and professional associations, and individuals; by government grants and contracts; and by private foundations. The Institute disseminates its work widely to the legal, business, and research communities, and to the general public. In accordance with RAND policy, all Institute research products are subject to peer review before publication. ICJ publications do not necessarily reflect the opinions or policies of the research sponsors or of the ICJ Board of Overseers.

For additional information about the Institute for Civil Justice, contact:
Robert T. Reville, Director
RAND Institute for Civil Justice
1700 Main Street, P.O. Box 2138
Santa Monica, CA 90407-2138
Phone: (310) 393-0411 x6786; Fax: (310) 451-6979
E-mail: Robert_Reville@rand.org; Web: www.rand.org/icj/

CALIFORNIA COMMISSION ON HEALTH AND SAFETY AND WORKERS' COMPENSATION

EMPLOYER MEMBERS

Jill Dulich, Regional Director, Marriott International, *Appointed by Governor*

Kristen Schwenkmeyer, Secretary-Treasurer, Gordon & Schwenkmeyer, *Appointed by Senate*

Robert B. Steinberg, Esq., Sr. Partner, Rose, Klein & Marias, *Appointed by Assembly*

John Wilson (retired), Schools Excess Liability Fund, *Appointed by Governor*

LABOR MEMBERS

Allen Davenport, Director of Government Relations, S.E.I.U. California State Council, *Appointed by Speaker of the Assembly*

Leonard McLeod, Finance Chair, California Correctional Peace Officers Association, *Appointed by Governor*

Tom Rankin, President, California Labor Federation, *Appointed by Senate*

Darrel (Shorty) Thacker, Central District Manager, Northern California, Council of Carpenters, *Appointed by Governor*

EXECUTIVE OFFICER

Christine Baker

For more than two decades, legislators, stakeholders, and litigants have complained that the process by which disputed workers' compensation claims in California are adjudicated and resolved has become ponderously slow, too expensive, and plagued by a lack of consistency from office to office, from judge to judge, and from case to case. In response to these concerns, the Commission on Health and Safety and Workers' Compensation (CHSWC), an independent state commission charged with monitoring and evaluating the California workers' compensation system, provided funding to the RAND Institute for Civil Justice (ICJ) to conduct a top-to-bottom review of the workers' compensation courts in the state.

This document is an Executive Summary of the comprehensive report resulting from that study. The full report—*Improving Dispute Resolution for California's Injured Workers* (RAND MR-1425-ICJ, 2003)—is contained on the CD included with this document. Printed copies of the full report can be purchased on request from RAND Distribution Services (Telephone: 310-451-7002; Fax: 310-451-6915; e-mail: order@rand.org).

CONTENTS

We would like to thank the California Commission on Health and Safety and Workers' Compensation for providing support for this research. The ongoing guidance of Christine Baker, the Executive Officer of the Commission, was much appreciated. Retired Workers' Compensation Judge Tom McBirnie acted as liaison with project staff and was an invaluable resource. Retired Workers' Compensation Judge Larry Swezey also provided us with his insightful comments and extensive knowledge of the system.

We are also grateful to the study's Resource and Advisory Committee, which consisted of several volunteer attorneys, judges, and California Division of Workers' Compensation (DWC) staff members from across the state, all of whom contributed their thoughts and the benefit of their experiences throughout the study. Their contributions and criticisms gave the authors an invaluable education and grounded the end result in reality.

We also thank the administrative staffs of the CHSWC, the DWC, and the Workers' Compensation Appeals Board (WCAB), who never hesitated to answer our questions or provide sometimes-sensitive data upon demand. No matter where we went, we found local attorneys and litigants, clerks, secretaries, hearing reporters, Information & Assistance Officers, disability raters, vocational rehabilitation staff, and others more than willing to take the time to participate freely in interviews and discussions whenever asked. We would also like to thank all the judges who agreed to participate in a burdensome weeklong time study.

Attorneys Diana Balabanian and Elena Mavros tackled the demanding job of poring over nearly 1,000 case files over a period of six weeks in order to extract much-needed data for this project. Despite sometimes grueling travel demands, they performed their jobs admirably and without complaint.

Professor Edward M. Welch (Director of the Workers' Compensation Center at Michigan State University), Dr. James S. Kakalik (former analyst for the RAND Institute for Civil Justice), and the Honorable Joel Gomberg (Workers' Compensation Judge for the Oakland DWC office and CHSWC staff consultant) all provided helpful criticisms and comments in their formal review of this report. We value their suggestions and hope that we have responded appropriately.

Finally, we would especially like to acknowledge the contributions of the entire California workers' compensation community who regularly mailed, e-mailed, phoned, or personally delivered their comments, suggestions, and personal experiences, without which the study would have been woefully incomplete.

California's 90-year-old workers' compensation system is designed to provide injured workers immediate and speedy relief without resorting to a formal trial. Instead of involving judges and the civil courts, injured workers may simply file a claim through a no-fault, administrative process.

In theory, the process for delivering workers' compensation benefits, such as medical care, replacement of lost wages, and vocational rehabilitation services, is precisely defined in the California Labor Code and other regulations and is mostly automatic. In reality, however, disputes often arise over issues such as whether an injury in fact occurred at work, whether medical treatment is necessary, and the extent to which an injury poses long-term consequences for the worker. All such disputes are resolved in a single forum: the Workers' Compensation Appeals Board (WCAB). Of the one million workers' compensation claims filed in California every year, about 200,000 end up at the WCAB.

For more than 20 years, however, the workers' compensation courts increasingly have been perceived as a weak link in the workers' compensation system. As early as 1981, the courts had become so bogged down with cases that some observers used the word "crisis" to describe the situation. What were once regarded as premium judicial services provided by the state's oldest social insurance system had become so problem-filled that a number of observers felt that the system was no longer serving the public interest.

Today, the workers' compensation courts are criticized primarily for three reasons: They are slow in reaching decisions, litigation is increasingly expensive, and the courts' procedures and actions have little consistency statewide. These problems have become so acute that they threaten to undermine the foundation of the entire workers' compensation system—a "social contract" by which injured workers give up their rights to seek damages in a civil court of law in exchange for compensation that is both swift and certain.

STUDY OBJECTIVES AND APPROACH

To address this situation, the California state legislature passed several comprehensive workers' compensation reform bills in recent years that, among other things, called for a top-to-bottom review of the courts. When all these bills were vetoed by the governor for budgetary and other reasons, the Commission on Health and Safety and Workers' Compensation (CHSWC), an independent state commission charged with monitoring and evaluating the California workers' compensation system, sought another avenue for conducting this review. The commission provided funding to the RAND Institute for Civil Justice (ICJ) to conduct a comprehensive analysis of the trial-level operations of the WCAB and the support and supervision of those operations provided by the California Division of Workers' Compensation (DWC). The ICJ study team focused on how the courts work, why they work the way they do, and how they can be improved.

The study team adopted a multifaceted approach that the ICJ has used successfully in other judicial process studies. The team members analyzed an on-line database compiled by the DWC that includes more than a million workers' compensation cases; they reviewed case files for nearly 1,000 claims to identify the key factors and events influencing how those claims were handled; and they visited many of the branch offices of the WCAB throughout the state to gain a better understanding of the processes used in litigating workers' compensation cases. The ICJ study team also conducted intensive site visits at six representative courts and asked all the judges in those courts to record how they spent their time over the course of a week. In addition, the study team interviewed a range of participants in the California workers' compensation system, including attorneys, judges, clerks, secretaries, hearing reporters, litigants, and others, and team members sat in on many conferences and trials.

Armed with this information, the research team analyzed the causes of delay in the resolution of workers' compensation disputes, the reasons for the high costs of litigation, and why procedures are inconsistent across the state. The study team found that the main problems afflicting the courts stem from decades of underfunding in the areas of staffing and technological improvements. Staff shortages affect every aspect of court operations and every part of the litigation process. The outmoded computer system of the DWC exacerbates the courts' problems because the system requires enormous duplication of data entry and has very limited capacity for caseload management or effective calendaring. These problems lead to delays, increase the private costs of prosecuting and defending cases, and create obstacles to reforming the outdated and contradictory rules and procedures that guide the courts.

In addition to a number of specific recommendations on policies and procedures designed to address these problems, the study team had three main recommendations:

- Provide realistic funding to fill every staff position that was authorized in 2001, assuming demands on the workers' compensation system remain at 2001 levels.

- Implement a complete overhaul of the courts' technological infrastructure without reducing short-term staffing levels.

- Conduct a comprehensive review, refinement, and coordination of all procedural rules governing the workers' compensation dispute resolution process.

A DISTINCTIVE SYSTEM OF JUSTICE

Approximately 180 trial judges in 25 local offices across California are at the heart of the state's workers' compensation dispute resolution system. The judges' judicial authority stems from the seven independent commissioners of the Workers' Compensation Appeals Board who are appointed by the governor and confirmed by the California Senate. While these commissioners have full power to review the trial judges' decisions, they have no direct supervisory control over the day-to-day operations of those judges. That authority rests with the Division of Workers' Compensation, a part of the California Department of Industrial Relations. The judges are employees of the DWC, along with the clerks, secretaries, hearing reporters, and other support staff in the local offices. DWC administrators decide where the judges will hold court, the size of the hearing rooms, the judges' work hours, and the quantity and type of staff support provided to the judges. The administrators of the DWC, along with the commissioners of the WCAB, are also responsible for developing the rules and policies used throughout the dispute resolution process.

Taken together, the WCAB and DWC are sometimes referred to as "The People's Court" because the litigant pool is so diverse and the courts' procedures are so informal that workers often represent themselves. It is a distinctive system for dispute resolution: A high-volume tribunal that never uses juries, operates under relatively relaxed rules of evidence, and has exclusive jurisdiction over most work injury disputes in this state. Judges must approve all settlements between injured workers and insurers and must also approve workers' attorney's fees. Rather than simply acting as a state agency's administrative law court, the WCAB is a fully functioning trial court of limited jurisdiction. Moreover, it functions as part of a much larger system of treating and compensating work injuries and returning employees back to the workplace as quickly as possible. To this end, judges are asked to construe the law liberally with the overriding purpose of extending legally entitled benefits to injured workers and are asked to do so "expeditiously, inexpensively, and without encumbrance of any character."[1]

As noted earlier, disputes over every aspect of the workers' compensation system are an ongoing fact of life. Participants in the workers' compensation process routinely differ over, for example, whether an injury did in fact arise from work activities, whether medical treatment is required at all, whether particular types of treatments are necessary and who will provide them, the extent of an employee's injuries and the long-term impact those injuries will have on his or her ability to make a living, whether the injured employee's condition has stabilized enough to be precisely evaluated, the amount and

---

[1]California Constitution, Article 14 ("Labor Relations"), Section 4.

duration of any cash benefits, whether vocational rehabilitation or ongoing medical care will be needed in the future, and many other critical issues. Unless these disputes are dropped or resolved informally, the parties must turn to the WCAB for adjudication.

To invoke the jurisdiction of the WCAB, a worker typically files an Application for Adjudication. No judicial action is automatically triggered by this filing; often, the application is submitted shortly after the injury has taken place but long before the worker's medical condition has stabilized—i.e., before the effects of any long-term disability can be evaluated.

After the worker and the employer or insurer are in a position to assess the future impact of an injury, settlement negotiations can then take place. If a negotiated resolution is not possible, either side in the dispute may then file a Declaration of Readiness to request that the case be placed in the queue for a future trial. The first event that follows the filing of the declaration, however, is the Mandatory Settlement Conference. This conference is designed to promote settlement with judicial assistance. If a settlement is not reached, a date must be set for a trial in the immediate future. If the case goes to trial, the judge will likely hear testimony from a handful of witnesses, but the judge's decision will be based primarily upon written medical evaluations submitted by each side.

The judge's decision will be issued days or even months after the trial. If either party disputes the outcome, that party can file a Petition for Reconsideration with the WCAB's commissioners for review. If at any point in this process the parties reach a settlement, they must submit the agreement to a trial judge for formal approval.

ADDRESSING THE CAUSES OF DELAY

As mentioned earlier, the workers' compensation system is different from the traditional civil law tort system in that injured workers give up their right to seek unlimited damages in exchange for swift and certain compensation and a promise to rapidly adjudicate any disputes that arise from their claims. To enforce this social bargain, California state law requires the courts to adhere to two specific time limits within the dispute process: The courts must hold an initial conference within 30 days from the time a party asks to have the case placed on the trial track through the filing of a Declaration of Readiness, and the courts must hold the trial within 75 days of the party's request.

The figure on this page shows the average amount of time, from 1995 to 2000, that cases took to get to conference and trial following the initial request to have them placed on the trial track. Although these averages, particularly the number of days to trial, have improved over the past few years, the reason for that improvement is primarily the decline in the number of new case filings from the peak numbers in the early 1990s, rather than more-efficient practices. Today, even with the reduced demand placed upon the courts, the time that it takes to hold both the conference and trial is much longer than the amount of time allowed by law.

What are the reasons for the courts' failure to meet the California legislature's mandates? As discussed next, the ICJ study team concluded that the causes of delays in holding conferences are quite different from the causes of delays in going to trial.

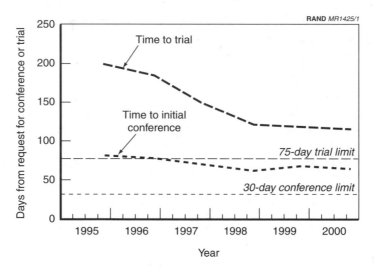

Average Time to Initial Conference and Trial, 1995–2000

Delays in Getting to Conference

The ICJ study team found understaffing to be the most important factor behind the slow pace in scheduling conferences. Most key positions in the California workers' compensation courts have been severely understaffed for years, with the most serious understaffing problem at the support-staff level: Clerks are in very short supply.

Overall, DWC local offices actually staff only about 70 percent of the number of authorized clerical-support positions because of a combination of insufficient funds for hiring, noncompetitive salaries, and high turnover rates. Some offices are operating with only half the number of authorized clerks. Because workers' compensation cases generate a great deal of paperwork, a chronic shortage of clerks creates a serious bottleneck in the system, particularly in getting cases to the initial conference stage. Clerks must review pleadings for compliance with legal requirements, enter relevant information into a computerized database, calendar conferences and trials, deal with questions from the public, perform most file management tasks, archive older cases, and perform a host of other duties. Because of understaffing and the heavy workload of the average clerk, it is not uncommon for an office's clerical staff to take 30 days just to process the request for trial and schedule a date for the initial conference. In other words, this step alone can consume all the time legally allotted to hold the Mandatory Settlement Conference.

As a result, the study team recommends that DWC administrators give top priority to hiring, training, and retaining clerks. Hiring and retention can be improved by slightly increasing clerks' pay to make it commensurate with the clerks' responsibilities and comparable with staff pay at other administrative law courts in the state.

The high clerical turnover rate makes retaining the clerks' supervisors vital to the courts' efficient operations. However, because lead clerks (i.e., supervisors) make less money than judges' secretaries do, they tend to leave their positions as soon as they find an opportunity for an intraoffice promotion. To address this problem, the study team also recommends that the clerical supervisor at each DWC local office be paid as much as judges' secretaries.

The hiring and retention measures that the study team recommends will require making changes to the state's traditional budgeting practices, which currently provide only 79 percent of the funds required to fully staff all existing authorized positions (including clerks, judges, secretaries, and other staff members) at the workers' compensation courts. The study team also recommends that the DWC take aggressive steps to minimize workers' compensation–related vacancies among its own staff and to improve the clerical training process.

Delays in Getting to Trial

The sources of delay in getting claims to trial are another matter. Judicial resource levels contribute to delay, but they do not fully explain why trials are not being held within the mandated 75-day time limit. Here, the study points to the behavior of judges, particularly judges who manage their personal trial calendars in counterproductive ways, or who liberally grant continuances, or who have not developed good case management or trial decisionmaking skills.

Judges have the ability to slow the pace of litigation in some offices by underscheduling the number of trials they hear or by freely granting continuances on the day of the hearing, sometimes postponing trial dates indefinitely. Although workers' compensation trials are traditionally very brief (with in-court testimony typically lasting two hours or less), the study showed that judges spend about four hours working on a case following the trial for every hour of testimony heard during the trial. This additional time is spent drafting a required summary of all the evidence heard, reviewing medical reports, writing a lengthy opinion, and frequently responding to an appeal—tasks not normally performed by civil court judges who, for the most part, preside over trials but do not decide cases. Preparing for trial adds yet more hours to a judge's workload for each hearing.

Therefore, one can understand why judges would try to minimize the number of trials they conduct to allow enough time for their other duties. But some judges carry this practice to an extreme. The underscheduling and questionable continuance practices of a few judges can extend the entire trial calendar for all other judges in that office.

The study team proposes several reforms to mitigate problems related to trial scheduling:

- First, when offices experience difficulties in getting trials scheduled within 45 days of the initial conference (especially if this situation appears to be limited to certain judges), then the office should consider moving to a system in which a judge other than the conference judge is typically assigned to handle the trial following the initial conference. The study team acknowledged that such procedural changes should be evaluated to determine if they actually increase efficiency and whether they should be adopted more widely.

- Second, judges should not be allowed to continue a morning trial to another day just because the trial was not completed by noon.

- Third, DWC local offices should review the formulas they use for trial calendaring to ensure some limited amount of overbooking. Scheduling slightly more trials than a judge can actually hear in one day is justified because many, if not most, of the cases will be settled before they reach trial. While the post-trial demands on a judge's time that each hearing requires should be considered when refining the trial calendaring formulas, making sure that a trial is held as soon as possible in every instance should be considered the shared responsibility of all judges in an office.

- Finally, a more flexible and efficient "rollover" policy would allow overbooked cases that failed to settle to be quickly reassigned to available judges on the day of a trial, a change that would also help fill some judges' occasionally empty trial calendars.

The study team also identified another cause of trial delays: Some judges take an unreasonable amount of time to submit decisions after a hearing. The study team found that, in some instances, judges took more than three months to reach a decision, even though 30 days is the maximum time established by statute. Even among judges in the same office with about the same workloads, there were wide disparities in the time they took to issue a decision. Interviews with secretaries and hearing reporters who work with judges who were slow to submit their decisions suggested that those judges simply lacked the necessary organizational and time-management skills.

One of the study team's most important recommendations is that judges need more formal training in how to perform the tasks required of them. Most new judges come from the ranks of attorney-advocates and therefore are already familiar with the world of workers' compensation law and practice. But new judges often have little experience in efficient note-taking during testimony, promoting settlements between contentious parties, managing a crowded conference calendar, issuing decisions quickly and competently following trial, and writing a well-reasoned opinion. As a result, some judges operate in the same inefficient way year after year because they have not been offered alternatives on how to manage their caseloads or streamline various tasks.

The study also suggests that each presiding judge (the supervising judge at each DWC local office) be firmly committed to cutting delays. In so doing, the presiding judges should spend more time mentoring the judges they supervise, make greater efforts to monitor judicial performance, and look for good case-management skills in candidates for judge positions.

REDUCING UNNECESSARY LITIGATION COSTS

The study team found that the permissive attitude of some judges in granting continuances at conferences and granting requests for postponements on the day of trial not only slows down the overall judicial process, it results in repeated appearances by counsel over the life of a drawn-out dispute. Every subsequent court date can be costly to defendants who must pay their counsel for each court appearance (even if the matter is continued), costly to workers' attorneys who have only a limited amount of time to devote to each case, and costly to workers who must take a day off from their jobs each time they have to appear in court.

The study team found that most of the continuances granted at the initial conferences were not issued to help the parties finalize an impending settlement; instead, they were granted as the result of a party waiting until the last minute to make a claim that the case was not ready for trial. It is not uncommon for attorneys to examine a case file for the first time right before a conference. Because all future discovery is cut off after a trial date is formally set at the end of the conference, an attorney who has not reviewed a case for more than a few minutes may look for an excuse to request a delay through a continuance or through an order to take the case off the trial calendar. Moreover, an attorney who is not yet familiar with a file is less effective in settlement negotiations (the primary purpose of the initial conference) and often fails to obtain authority to settle the case in advance of the initial conference.

Curtailing last-minute postponements may be the single most important step to reducing litigation costs. The authors of this report make several proposals to help reduce the number of such postponements:

- Other than those related to illnesses and emergencies, continuances and removals from the trial calendar should be considered only if specific requests are made in writing, filed, and served within a specific number of days after the filing of the Declaration of Readiness. By forcing parties in a case to review the case file at the time the request for trial is made, the settlement process at the initial conference is more likely to be successful, thereby avoiding a trial and reducing costs.

- More proactive case management is needed for cases that are continued. No continuance should be granted without (1) the parties in a case being given a specific date to return, (2) the judge explicitly detailing in the file the reasons for granting the request, and (3) orders being issued describing what is to be done to get the case back on track. Many judges currently grant requests for postponement without requiring any other next step, causing the case to drift into "judicial limbo" and sometimes into an endless cycle of costly delays.

- Judges must stop granting requests for postponements on the day of trial in all but the most extraordinary circumstances. If a judge is faced with more trials than can be heard in a single day, the presiding judge should be immediately informed and the case rolled over to another judicial officer, if possible.

MAKING PROCEDURES MORE UNIFORM

One of the main complaints heard from practitioners and judges is that the rules governing practice in workers' compensation courts across the state are unclear and inconsistent. These concerns are not surprising given that the controlling rules and procedures are derived from a wide variety of sources, including the California Labor Code, WCAB Rules, DWC Administrative Director Rules, and the DWC/

WCAB Policy & Procedural Manual. Because the rules are sometimes contradictory, vague, confusing, or convoluted, many local offices and judges invent their own procedures or evaluative criteria, creating a hodgepodge of largely unwritten local practices across the state.

In addressing the issue of uniformity, the authors of this report make a distinction between the pretrial and trial litigation phases. The trial already has built-in procedures that encourage uniformity. The judge's production of a comprehensive summary of evidence presented at trial, the use of detailed and organized reports for the presentation of medical evidence as opposed to only brief oral testimony, the relatively unhurried post-trial decisionmaking process, the requirement that the judge must clearly document the reasoning behind his or her decision, and the ability of litigants to easily appeal on questions of fact rather than solely on questions of law are all practices that help to insure high-quality trial outcomes. But such safeguards do not exist for pretrial decisions and case management.

The study team found wide variation in judicial actions and behavior prior to trial, including how judges handle continuances and other postponements, the standards they use to decide whether proposed settlements comply with the law, and the criteria they use to approve attorneys' fees. In most instances, the reasons for the variation in behavior appeared to stem from the rules themselves; often, there was simply no clear and unambiguous guidance on the proper course of action in a case.

To promote greater uniformity and efficiency in the rules governing practice in the workers' compensation courts, the study team recommends a coordinated and long-term effort by both the WCAB and the DWC to (1) review the various sources of the rules, (2) eliminate or correct language that is no longer relevant or that is vague or confusing, (3) highlight the rules that are clear and straightforward, (4) provide supplemental commentary to act as guideposts in making decisions, and (5) revise the forms and procedures accordingly. This review should be conducted not only by WCAB commissioners and DWC administrators but also by judges and attorneys to make sure that the new rules will work in actual practice. This review process is the single most important step that can be taken immediately to improve uniformity prior to trial. While progress in this area has been made recently, much more is needed.

RETHINKING A NUMBER OF PAST REFORM PROPOSALS

While the study team has proposed a number of recommendations for change, the team also explored several prominent reform proposals frequently cited in the debate about California's workers' compensation courts. The study team found that those proposals might be unnecessary, ill advised, costly, or premature. They include proposals to (1) implement a new automated case management system without first increasing staff levels and performing a comprehensive review of regulations, (2) create a new upper-level system-wide position of Court Administrator, (3) eliminate specific judicial tasks in order to reduce judges' workloads, and (4) require an additional case status conference at the outset of every dispute. The following section presents the pros and cons of each proposal.

Updating the Computer System Without Adequate Staffing, Funding, and Planning

We noted earlier that the DWC's computer system is woefully outdated, consumes enormous staff resources, and is in need of an overhaul. However, moving to an automated case management system and electronic filing of claims and pleadings without supplemental funding and staffing will likely lead to significant and costly disruptions in case processing in the short term and a flawed upgrade in the long term. The considerable expense of designing and installing a new system would be incurred at a time when the workers' compensation courts clearly do not have enough available staff at their local offices. In the current fiscal environment, taking such a step to fund the implementation of updated technology would likely reduce personnel levels even further, a situation that could have disastrous consequences for litigants.

Moving to an automated system without first reviewing existing regulations and policies might also "cement in" current inefficient practices, contradictory regulations, and out-of-date pleadings. While the study team emphasizes that the current electronic case management system is a source of much wasted time and effort, and recommends that the groundwork for implementation of an updated system (such as exploring design alternatives and seeking supplemental state funding) be initiated as soon as possible, they caution, however, that a significant diversion of funds or staffing for this purpose could prove to be counterproductive. Adequate staffing, funding, and planning for future technological upgrades should be implemented simultaneously.

Creating a New Court Administrator Position

Recent legislation[2] signed by Governor Gray Davis in 2002 establishes the new position of a systemwide court administrator who will be charged with expediting the judicial process, supervising judges, and establishing uniform court procedures. The study team found that even if the court administrator's position had more-sweeping powers than those eventually approved in AB 749 (as were envisioned in an earlier version of the legislation), the position would still be unlikely to address the critical causes of delay, high litigation costs, and contradictory regulations identified in the team's analysis. In fact, the study team found that the court administrator would have had no greater supervisory powers than the administrative director of the DWC has today, nor would the position as it was originally envisioned have had additional authority to increase resources or make judges adhere to deadlines and other rules. Moreover, establishing the new position and staffing the court administrator's office would likely shift resources away from the lowest-paid positions in the DWC, the department level that needs increased staff resources the most.

Eliminating Two Specific Judicial Tasks

The ICJ study team also rejected the idea of eliminating two long-standing judicial requirements—the summary of evidence and the review of all settlements—despite the hours of labor they require of already overworked judges. The study found that summaries of evidence, which are typically prepared from copious handwritten notes and are very time-consuming, provide a great benefit to the

---

[2]California Assembly Bill No. 749, 2001–2002 Reg. Sess., chaptered February 19, 2002.

decisionmaking process and substantial savings in private litigation costs. Judges currently are also required to review all proposed settlements. Although about 15 percent of a judge's time is spent reviewing proposed agreements, the study team found that the effort expended on this task was justified because so many complicated cases are resolved by workers themselves without the assistance of an attorney. Even in cases involving attorneys on both sides, judicial review helps to protect the interests of lien claimants who do not always participate directly in the settlement process.

Requiring an Initial Status Conference

The study team found the "one conference, one trial" litigation model (currently utilized by the WCAB) to be a reasonable one, and did not endorse the proposal that an initial "status conference" be required to identify potential problems early in a case. While such a practice may be justified in particular cases, the study team found that the administrative costs for adopting this proposal statewide would be overwhelming.

CONCLUSIONS

What is the main factor behind the problems of the so-called People's Court? The study team found little evidence to support a number of widely held views on this question.

It is not that the WCAB and DWC administration is indifferent to the system's problems or is resistant to reform; in fact, administrators appear to be consumed by problems of chronic staff shortages and have little opportunity to address systemwide problems.

It is not that current rules and policies are at the heart of the courts' problems and simply need to be modified to achieve more prompt resolutions and fewer court appearances. Revamping the rules would do little on its own to correct the courts' most pressing problems.

And, above all, it is not that the courts have excess funds that contribute to waste and inefficiencies, and therefore the courts need to be underfunded to make them run "leaner and meaner." The full report on this study lays that theory to rest with a comprehensive description of the inefficiencies created by inadequate budgets, which have resulted in high staff turnover, the inability to attract competent personnel, outmoded computing equipment, the lack of a modern case management information system, packing of initial conference calendars, and judges being overloaded with trial work. All of these problems are symptoms of a system that is failing on its promise to deliver swift and equitable compensation for workplace injuries.

The study team concludes that the primary source of the complaints from the workers' compensation community is the chronic funding shortage, which has hampered hiring, training, and technological improvements for decades. Year after year of scrambling to provide local offices with the bare minimum of staff has prevented DWC administration from addressing long-term needs, most notably the long-overdue upgrade of the courts' information technology infrastructure. Ironically, the courts' computer system has made staff shortages more acute because the outmoded system requires a great deal of duplicate data entry. Its inability to automatically schedule future conferences and trials means that clerks must laboriously perform the task of calendaring the exact same way that they have for decades, resulting in delays in scheduling initial conferences and in costly calendaring conflicts for litigants. Moreover, the system is so old that it offers little help as a management tool to more efficiently allocate judicial resources. Yet, replacing this system has not been possible given the gaping holes in office staffing that have been the status quo in nearly every fiscal year in recent memory.

In the face of long-term funding and staffing shortages, procedural uniformity also has become more difficult to achieve. To meet legislatively mandated time limits for case processing, some local offices, for example, have dispensed with certain aspects of pleading review that the offices believe consume unjustifiable amounts of staff resources. And plans for uniform training manuals for staff have been on the back burner for years because lead clerks and lead secretaries cannot be spared to draft the documents. The problem of non-uniformity is not likely to go away anytime soon: The assignment of judges and administrators to the much-needed long-term task of reviewing conflicting or ambiguous procedural regulations has been made extremely difficult in a fiscal environment such as the current one.

Most important, insufficient staffing levels can diminish the quality of justice. Judges who are facing considerable workload demands from every trial over which they preside may prefer the idea of granting requests for continuances, however questionable they may be, over more prompt resolutions that would add yet more work to their plates. When trials do take place, a judge's careful and deliberate review of the record when making a decision may not be possible because of other equally pressing demands on the judge's time. Presiding judges are unable to closely supervise the work of their trial judges, as long as those presiding judges have to handle a nearly equal share of each office's routine caseload, a complaint the research team heard again and again from both defense counsel and injured workers' attorneys. Resource shortages have also prevented initial and ongoing training of trial judges. As a result, there is a great disparity in the knowledge and abilities among those who are asked to be the final arbiters in this system.

SUMMARY OF RECOMMENDATIONS

The ICJ study team developed three main recommendations to address the problems confronting California's workers' compensation courts, in addition to a number of specific recommendations on workers' compensation system policies and procedures.

Main Recommendations

1. **Provide adequate funding to fill every position that was authorized in 2001, assuming that demands on the system remain at 2001 levels.** Rather than calling for more positions, the study team found that staffing levels authorized in 2001 reasonably match current caseloads. But the traditional practice of state government has been to provide the DWC with just 79 percent of the funds needed to fill all authorized positions. This study calls for addressing this built-in shortfall and filling *all* authorized positions. Adequate funding also includes adjustments in the salaries for specific job classifications, most notably for clerks and their supervisors, which need to be high enough to attract and retain qualified recruits. Some offices, for example, are currently operating at half the number of clerks for which they are authorized, a staffing level

far below what was needed to process the enormous amount of paperwork generated in 2001.

If demands placed on the workers' compensation system increase from 2001 levels as a result of population growth, changes in the rules for workers' compensation, or for any other reason, the number of authorized positions would have to increase as well. Ultimately, adequate funding must be made available each year, and not simply as a one-time fix.

2. **Implement a complete overhaul of the court's technological infrastructure without reducing short-term staff levels.** The DWC Claims Adjudication On-Line System (CAOLS) used for case management purposes is woefully outdated. CAOLS clearly is a source of much waste and delay, and it should be replaced. Any such system replacement or overhaul, however, must be in addition to, and not in exchange for, adequate funding for current personnel requirements. Only after a modern case management system is in place, and the long-touted benefits of electronic filing come to pass, can the number of support positions be reduced, as well as the costs of administering the workers' compensation courts. Until then, those responsible for resource allocation must be willing to support full staffing levels *and* the costs of the infrastructure upgrade.

3. **Conduct a comprehensive review, refinement, and coordination of all procedural rules.** Existing WCAB Rules, DWC Administrative Director Rules, directives contained in the DWC/WCAB Policy & Procedural Manual, and the set of official pleadings all must be updated, coordinated, and made consistent by a standing committee composed of judges, WCAB commissioners, DWC administrators, practitioners, and other members of the workers' compensation community. A key goal of this group should be to minimize variation in interpreting procedural rules, including what constitutes good cause for granting continuances and orders to take a case out of the trial queue. The commissioners of the WCAB have recently taken some steps toward the goal of conducting a comprehensive review, but an even greater effort needs to be made.

The review process must also be ongoing so that no rule or regulation becomes so irrelevant or unrealistic that it ends up being routinely ignored by judges and practitioners. As with the need for adequate funding, a one-time review would be nothing more than a temporary fix.

Specific Recommendations

The study team also proposes a number of specific recommendations to address the problems faced by the California workers' compensation courts. Some of those recommendations are listed here. For the complete list of recommendations, see the full report on this study (*Improving Dispute Resolution for California's Injured Workers*, RAND MR-1425-ICJ) contained on this document's companion CD.

Recommendations Concerning Judicial Responsibilities and Training

- Presiding judges must view the goal of insuring the prompt, uniform, and streamlined resolution of the office's caseload as their primary duty. Their close monitoring of the actions of trial judges and support staff is critical to insuring that both the letter and spirit of administrative policy and formal regulations are carried out.

- Judges need more than an extensive knowledge of workers' compensation rules and case law to effectively carry out their duties. They must have the necessary skills for performing the case management and decisionmaking aspects of their jobs. The existing training in this area is inadequate and needs improvement.

- New training programs for judges should focus on the best ways for them to manage individual caseloads and to issue trial decisions rapidly.

Recommendations Concerning Conference and Trial Scheduling

- Trial calendaring should be done by clerical staff and not by the judge who presides over the Mandatory Settlement Conference (MSC).

- If local offices are having problems with scheduling and completing trials within a reasonable period of time following the MSC, then the office should consider moving to a system in which a judge *other* than the conference judge is typically assigned to handle the trial following the initial conference. In such a system, the trial judge assignment is generally made according to which judge has the next available open trial slot. The DWC should evaluate the effects of any office's change in their policy regarding trial judge assignment, both for assessing whether the new policy should be adopted systemwide and for determining if the switch has in fact achieved its goals at the office in question.

- Calendaring formulas should be monitored and regularly adjusted to ensure that each judge has a sufficient and balanced trial workload. Better procedures are needed for shifting cases from overbooked judges on a trial day to other judges with a lighter trial schedule. A mandatory "roll call" at the beginning of the daily trial calendar should aid judges in determining whether they can hear all the trials scheduled for them that day. The presiding judge should be regularly updated with information about canceled and anticipated trials each morning.

- If offices are having problems with scheduling and completing trials within a reasonable time, they should consider switching to a single day-long trial calendar rather than using separate calendars for the morning and afternoon.

Recommendations Concerning Postponements

- Except under extraordinary circumstances, judges at conferences should grant continuances or orders to take a case off the trial calendar only if they receive formal, written requests from the moving party before the initial conference detailing the reasons for the postponement.

- Unless they are associated with an *impending* settlement, day-of-trial requests for continuances or orders to take a case off the trial calendar should rarely be granted. If granted, counsel should be required to serve their respective clients with a copy of the detailed order.

- No continuance or order taking a case off the trial calendar should be granted at a conference or trial without (1) setting a new date for the parties to return, (2) explaining to the parties in writing why the delay was granted, and (3) outlining what is to be accomplished during the delay. A litigant's failure to accomplish the promised tasks should be a subject of great concern to a judge.

Recommendations Concerning Settlements and Attorneys' Fees

- Judges should continue to review all proposed settlements. Judicial oversight is an important way to insure that the mission of the workers' compensation system is carried out under all circumstances.

- The standards for granting settlements, and the form those agreements can take, need to be more precisely defined to reduce frustration among the bar when attorneys request approval of proposed settlement agreements and to address the serious problem of nonuniform application of approval criteria.

- The criteria for the awarding of both attorneys' fees and deposition fees need to be more precisely defined to reduce frustration among the bar when attorneys make fee requests and to address the problem of nonuniform awards.

Recommendations Concerning Other Pretrial Matters

- The rules regarding preconference screening of Declarations of Readiness and the rules regarding any review of objections filed in response to those trial requests need to be clarified.

- The criteria for determining what constitutes availability of a representative with settlement authority need to be clarified, and judges should be given better guidance on what to do when a representative is not present or is not available.

Recommendations Concerning Trials

- If any trial decisions are pending for more than 30 days after the final receipt of all evidence in a case, the delay should be considered presumptive evidence that the judge has unfinished work in his or her daily duties. A delay of more than 60 days should be perceived as a clear sign that the judge requires additional training in the decisionmaking process.

- Judges should be allowed to adopt their original Opinion and Decision as a Report on Reconsideration if they certify that they have done a full review of the Petition for Reconsideration and have considered possible modifications to their decision.

Recommendations Concerning Technology and Administration

- Although a system for electronic filing of pleadings is clearly the model of the future, implementing such a system within the California workers' compensation courts is premature at this time. Electronic filing should become the standard method for filing documents with the WCAB only after the CAOLS has been completely replaced and the rules of practice and procedure have been reviewed and updated.

- A networked calendaring system for the scheduling of trials and conferences should be the top priority among new technological implementations. All clerks should be trained in the use of this system and should be able to operate it from any terminal within the district offices to avoid bottlenecks during absences. Litigants should be able to remotely provide potentially conflicting court dates to reduce scheduling problems.

A BLUEPRINT FOR THE FUTURE

The WCAB has become a focus of attention for those who feel that the entire California workers' compensation system has strayed from its original purpose of delivering swift and certain benefits through a user-friendly dispute resolution system that serves the interests of injured workers, employers, and other litigants.

This study suggests that if the way in which the courts operate continues to be plagued by unnecessary delays that frustrate injured workers and their employers, by unreasonable private and public litigation costs, and by unexpected outcomes due to idiosyncratic procedures, the California workers' compensation system is in fact failing to serve its statutory and historical mandate. The ICJ study team's recommendations offer a blueprint for judicial and administrative reform that will help the system to fulfill that mandate.